T0144951

Please READ to ME
Book 3

DOUGIE THE DOG

Betty "Beattie" Chandorkar

To order additional copies of this book, contact:
Xlibris
1-888-795-4274
www.Xlibris.com
Orders@Xlibris.com

Please READ to ME
Book 3

DOUGIE THE DOG

Betty "Beattie" Chandorkar

Hello, I am a stuffed dog who sits up proudly and am able to sing, sway my front legs, and tap one foot in time with music that I play. I was a rather unique toy when I arrived at the hospital to entertain–causing smiles from the patient, doctors, nurses, and care people.

I work on batteries, and when they are turned on, my tape plays "Singin' in the Rain." I sound very much like Gene Kelly, and they say I have a delightful personality.

My front legs hold a curled-up umbrella, which I move in time with the music and my dainty little toe tap-taps.

I am a cute little stuffed dog, all dressed up in a yellow plastic raincoat, a rain hat, and yellow booties.

The song is a catchy tune, so I sing my heart out to bring smiles to all.

> I'm singing in the rain (tap tap)
>
> Just singing in the rain (tap tap)
>
> What a glorious feeling
>
> I'm happy again (tap tap)

Many years have passed, and I now sit silently on a bedside table. My arms no longer sway back and forth, but I can still tap my little toe. Very few people come to enjoy my song, and I am very lonely.

The cleaning lady dusts around me, and BB, my hostess, does pat my head and say hello. At least I am not stuffed in a box somewhere. I love to entertain, and now I don't get many chances to perform.

One day a little toddler wandered into the bedroom. I guess I would waddle too if I had to walk on only two back legs. He was very young and packed with a bulky diaper. His name was Kevin, and he greeted me with a big smile. We were friends right away. He jabbered at me, but when I didn't answer, he picked me up by the ears!

"Oh no, not my ears!"

I am a heavy little toy, and my ears are very sensitive. We bounced along the hallway to a big room where the adults were having a cup of tea.

The sweet little boy chuckled with glee as he dragged me to meet his parents. He was so happy to have a "pal," and I shyly sat beside him, trying to look cute too. I did look smart in my little yellow raincoat and hat.

They loved my little song as I tapped to the music.

Kevin was given a slice of bread with jam—bright-red strawberry jam!

This kind little fellow had been taught to share—and he pushed his treat into my muzzle.

"Oh no, Kevin, I am a stuffed toy and I cannot open my mouth! My face and lovely raincoat are covered with jam!"

BB and Kevin's mother rushed about and wiped my face, my little coat, and spots on the carpet. Kevin trotted about to find other toys to pull about.

In the meantime, I sneaked a lick of jam and it was delicious!

As luck would have it, Kevin's father is a "fixer." Why can't I move my arms with the music?

Right away we were on the floor, and he was pulling up my raincoat. Oh my goodness! Just beside him was a big metal toolbox! He took out a chisel, a pair of pointed pliers, a little saw, and a big hammer!

I was now lying on my tummy and could see that horrible "hitting thing" looking so dangerous. What was the father doing to my back? I could hear the scissors cutting my fur, and there were bangs and snapping noises, but of course, I felt no pain.

All of them are now cheering! I have my back taped and covered again.

Now with new batteries and the switch turned on, I am singing. I can tap my toe and swing my arms! I am again a cute little dog who sings and dances.

What a relief—the big hammer has been put back into the toolbox.

Little Kevin gave me a big hug before he went home.

I have been sitting in the bedroom for many years. Everyone seems to be too busy to take the time to enjoy my song.

One day a tall man with a low voice picked me up so carefully. Yes, I knew him when he hugged me. It was Kevin! This time he carried me carefully to the big room to meet his wife and little baby daughter. This tiny child was cuddled in her basket, and I could see her hands flying about and her little feet kicking at the sides. She wasn't too interested when I was turned on and took the stage to sing and dance for my friend and his lovely wife.

At a later visit, this time the same little girl, now a toddler, found me in the bedroom and carefully carried me to the room where the adults were having tea. I did sing, sway my arms, and tap my toe, and she giggled just like her father did years ago.

But this time I was upstaged! This pretty little girl could sway her arms and tap both toes in time with the music! She even spun herself around and made a big bow at the end of the song! The adults all clapped and shouted in glee, but not for me!

How can I compete with this child star? How can I look cute when she is so pretty?

Oh, yes, I know. She won't be able to sing the words yet, so I can dance and sing and be the star of the show.

When I see her again, I'll teach her the words of my song, and we can act together.

We will be dancing and singing a duet!

I'm happy again!

ACTIVITIES

1. Some household chores are quite safe and simple. How do you wash out food stains in a rug, on clothes, or on floors?

2. Other repair jobs in your home should be done by trained workmen. List those you think would need professional help.

3. Most homes have a standard toolbox. Study those tools and have an adult show you how they are usually used. Be careful; some will be very sharp.

4. Velcro tape holds Dougie's raincoat closed. Use a magnifying glass to see how this tape replaces buttons.

5. What other articles in your home play music?

6. What other equipment needs batteries?

7. What is a duet? a solo? a quartet? a trio? Be careful with your answer!

8. At what age do children usually learn to walk? At what age do they learn to sing?

Printed in the United States
By Bookmasters